Voices of t...

A Celebration of Writing Contest Winners
2011-2012

Sponsored by
Endless Mountains Writing Project
With financial support from First Citizens National Bank

Editors
Nanci Werner-Burke, PhD
Dick Heyler

Published by

Pen & Publish

Bloomington, Indiana
(812) 837-9226
info@PenandPublish.com
www.PenandPublish.com

ISBN: 978-0-9842258-9-7

This book is printed on acid free paper.

Printed in the USA

Foreword

In his book, The Great Good Place, sociologist Ray Oldenburg (1991) categorizes the human experience as having three central sites or places; work, social, and home. While each person defines, understands, and values these three sites in varied ways, they remain the essential sites by which we manage the days that culminate into our lives.

With these three "great places" in mind, and the physical and technological changes that are occurring with lightning speed in our region and world, we set our theme for the annual Voices of the Twin Tiers Writing Contest as " A Sense of Place". This volume contains the winning entries from writers of all ages who reflected on the theme and produced written work that captures places and moments, memorializing them on the page.

While this volume celebrates these writers and their work, consider that as we shift more into a digital world, this print volume may be the only way these works are preserved.

Consider your own connections to the far past - a trunk of old love letters, worn journals and diaries, boxes and books of fading sepia photos on tin, all commemorating now-absent, passed ancestors and past times. A faded postcard may be the only connection you have to a great-grand parent, or a journal page may serve as an insight into what a long-departed aunt or uncle was thinking or doing on a particular day.

We are increasing turning to blogs rather than journals, to webfeeds more than printed newspapers. We keep photos stored on phones and memory cards rather than printing them. Today's writer texts and emails and communicates in real time with people across the world and across the table. For all of these means of communication, there are certainly advantages. New applications and literacies evolve constantly. One disadvantage, one thing that is lost, though, is the paper trail. The written and visual artifacts that remind us of how we were and who we have become are increasingly temporary, a flitter of light and pixels on a screen.

Servers crash, viruses invade hard drives and thumb drives get bent out of shape. Blogs get deleted, websites and domains wink out of sight as online accounts shift from free to paid. When this cloud bursts, we may be the first generation since the industrial revolution to not have a huge expanse of tangible written artifacts to archive our daily existence.

Here, though, in your hand, you hold a record of written thought that captures the thinking of a wide band of people in our region. Whether you read it and then use it to prop up the short leg on a wobbly table, it will still be there when the lights go out. The voices will be there, waiting to be heard, waiting to whisper, to shout, to scare and amuse. Open, and enjoy.

We are again indebted to First Citizens Bank for their financial support of our writing contest and of our community.

We thank these future English teachers at Mansfield University for their work in culling the first round of entries:
Amanda Cino
Jordan Hallock
Kaitlyn Hedgeland
Caitlin Johnson
Marta Knapp
Kaitlin Magni
Olivia Mishler

The Endless Mountains Writing Project team of teacher consultants who volunteered their time for the final round of judging:
Amy De Camp
Robin Glowatz
Dick Heyler
Lisa Higham
Jane Spohn

To EMWP teacher consultant Heather Manchester, who organized the entries so that they could be judge in a blind process and who followed up with our winning writers to gather information for their biographical blurbs, a prolonged shout-out.

Ongoing thanks to those teachers who made this contest a part of their work with students and who work daily to improve the teaching of writing and learning in our schools. Your daily passion and compassion is one of the last glues that bind our society.

Recognition and gratitude to Ruth Tonachel, both for her photographic contribution for the book cover and for her tireless work preserving the great spaces in our region with the Northern Tier Cultural Alliance.

And, of course, we thank our writers, who took a double-risk in putting words on the page and then turning those pages over for scrutiny and judging.

Table of Contents

An Overlook at the Forest
By Carter J.

The leaves of red,
green, and yellow I see in fall.
With crunching under my feet,
leaves of noise and a great oak tree.
The animals are as cute as can be like
the squirrels, chipmunks, caterpillars too.
An overlook at the forest for everyone to share,
a forest can be at any time nearly everywhere.
Now the sun sets and a beauty can be seen.
From a deep orange to a perfect pink
then the sun sets completely
and our overlook of the forest
sets to an end.

Carter J. is 9 years old, in third grade and loves to read. He has two brothers and likes doing activities with them. Carter wrote An Overlook at the Forest because he was inspired by the leaves of Fall. His favorite part about his work is the description of the animals of the forest because he used some pretty good descriptive words, in his opinion.

My Sense of Place
By Logan T.

My sense of place is on my dirt bike.
I taste dust when I am driving on the dirt path.
I taste mud when I am riding in the pasture.
My hands touch the clutch and throttle so I can go fast.
I smell fresh cut grass in the lawn.
Everybody around me smells rubber when do a burn-out.
Everyone sees a nice # 20 on my 80 Yamaha as I drive it down the road.
I hear a big motor and mud landing on my helmet.
My sense of place is on my dirt bike.

Logan T. likes dirt bikes. He lives in the country and loves riding in the pasture. Another hobby Logan enjoys is raising his chickens and ducks. He chose to write about dirt bikes because he enjoys riding them so much. Logan's favorite part was writing about touching the throttle and clutch.

3

My Sense of Place
By Evan K.

My sense of place is on my four wheeler.
I taste the mud and dirt that I fling up in the air.
When I drive down the road, I can hear fire in my
muffler.
Why do I hear the engine getting louder and louder?
My eyes can see all of the trees.
My sense of place is on my four wheeler.

*Evan K. is a 4th grader at Warren L. Miller Elementary
School. He lives on a family owned dairy farm and
likes to experience nature on his ATV.*

My Sense of Place
By Austin S.

My sense of place is a creek at my house
My sense of place smells like fish.
I see fish swimming under the water.
I touch rocks every now and then.
I am lifting rocks every now and then.
I taste the cool water on my tongue.
I hear the water slipping through the rocks.
My sense of place has a lot of views that are nice.
That is why my sense of place is the creek at my
house

Austin S. is 10 yrs old. He has twin sisters and a brother. He wrote about the creek because it's a place he likes to relax and have fun with his cousins. His favorite sentence is "My sense of place has a lot of views that are nice."

My Sense of Place
By Gilbert W.

My sense of place is a pricker bush.
Why do I smell cow manure? Because it is by my
dad's field.
Ace and I hear crackling in my pricker bush.
My sister and I taste prickers.
Why do I touch prickers? I am in a pricker bush!
Kayla and I see bears by our pricker bush.
That is why I like my pricker bush.

Gilbert W.is 9 years old and lives and works on his father's farm. He has an older brother, Ace, and an older sister, Kayla. He lives in Mansfield, Pennsylvania. Gilbert chose to write about a pricker bush because they are good places to hide. "Ace and I hear crackling in my pricker bush" is his favorite part in My Sense of Place.

My Sense of Place
By Abby P.

My sense of place is in my fort.
It gives me joy.
I see calming deer, birds, and chipmunks.
I hear hummingbirds it makes me feel joyful.
I touch the soft leaves.
I taste apples and raspberries and it makes me feel happy.
Sometimes I smell a stinky skunk, it makes me want to throw up.
That is why my fort is my sense of place.

Abby P. is 9 years old and lives in Mansfield, PA. She chose this topic because her fort in her back yard really is her favorite place. Abby plays with her little brother and her friends in her fort. She likes to make up stories about the animals she sees outside and draw them. Abby's favorite phrase is when she talks about the stinky smelly skunk and how it makes her want to throw up.

The Football Field
By Satchel M.

My favorite place is the football field. With its neat white lines. The metal bleachers with all kinds of people kids, adults, teenagers, and families of people on the field. The turf, it's so green and soft. When the sun shines on the turf it's so bright, and I love the gear: the white helmets, the black and gray shoulder pads, and the sharp cleats. I love the football with its nice pigskin texture, the elite stitching and it's a brown oval like a diamond. The crowd cheers and boos loudly and softly. The coaches yelling and giving pep talks. The concession stand with all kinds of flavorful varieties of food. Some days playing with clear blue sky and some days with rain soaking through our jerseys. Cheerleaders on the sideline for each team. The brick red track surrounding the field like a brick house in the middle of the forest. But my favorite thing about the football field is the thrill of getting a touchdown and scoring 6 points, that's the best part of the football field.

Satchel M. is 10 years old and goes to Lynch-Bustin Elementary in Athens, PA. He lives near a small lake and likes to spend time outdoors. He played Small Fry football for the first time in the fall and that inspired this piece.

Swim Chick on Race Day
By Catherine C.

The swimming pool is like home to me. I have spent so much time there. I know every little speck of the bottom of the pool better than my own best friend. I have been swimming on a competitive swim team since I was six years old. I know all the strokes and can swim them well. My most favorite stroke is the butterfly, which most people say is the hardest stroke.

I love to swim. Swimming has changed my life. You may want to know why. Swimming has given me confidence to get up on the tall starting blocks, swim my race the best I can, and to race against people I have never raced before. At the swim meets I socialize with other people, really get to know them, and have a fun time. My friend tells me there is a spot on my suit, then taps me on the nose when I look down. We laugh. The only thing is, when I get in the pool it's time to do my work, it's fun, but not all game time.

Swim meets really are fun, but in a competition I get really nervous especially right before the race. When I walk over to the starting blocks, I can see everybody cheering. I hear loud voices screaming "Come on Catherine, you can do it, you can do it!" I smell the chlorine, (which I personally do not like). I feel myself shaking with nervousness. 1 look at the size of some of the people I race, and they are huge and tall. My dad always says "it's not about the size of the dog in the fight; it's about the size of the fight in the dog." That means it doesn't matter how big or small you are, you can still be as fast or as good as them. I sing a song to myself before my race and think "I am going to win this race. I can do it." When the "starters" hit the buzzer I swim as fast as I can. When it's over I am out of breath. I look at where my competition is and for my time on the board. I may not always win or have a new best time, but I know there's always a next time. My dad says I am so proud of you. I smile.

Catherine C. is a fifth grade student at Warren L. Miller Elementary school in Mansfield, PA and she enjoys writing stories. She chose this topic because she enjoys writing about real life events. Her favorite sport is swimming and she swims on a local team called Northern Tier Aquatics (NTAQ). Her favorite pastime games are playing with her dog Bear and her sister Molly.

(untitled)
By K.C. B.

Looking up, sometimes I see, a white streak
heading across the sky.
Then I think of what the passengers must feel,
when whizzing so quickly by.
But then I remember (Oh silly me!)
I know what it's like to cross over the sea.
Ahhhhhh...
The feeling of soaring always makes me feel
pleased.
As we're inside a jet, safe from the breeze.
Enough about that though, I've got plenty of room!
So sit down, and grab some hot cocoa with a spoon!
I could explain the plane's many functions,
but that will most likely put you in a junction.
So I'll just explain the passenger's view.
The passenger is the big kahuna, the one who buys
the super-expensive drinks and souvenirs.
So if anyone interferes, the passenger will be
missing a snow-globe and the jet company will be
missing its $35!
One of the worst parts is if a baby's on board. At
first they're cute but next thing
you know, each one screams and hollers!
But enough about bitter things, let's get to the good
stuff.
As you sit in a seat, you'll immediately know that
it's as comfy as fluff.
Now with all the airplane knowledge you know,
on your next flight it may show!

*K.C. wrote this poem as a project in his enrichment
class. His teacher suggested they write about some*

place they like to be. K.C. has flown in planes several times and enjoys it quite a bit. His favorite part of the poem is about the over-expensive snow globe.

Winter Is On Its Way
By Joelle U.

Winter is on its way,
Leaves are beginning to fall,
The skies are becoming gray,
And the sunshine dull,
Without wearing a coat, children can no longer
play.

Apples are atop the ground,
Except for the breeze, you cannot hear a sound.
We will soon get our first frost,
Many fruits and such will be lost.
The geese will begin to flee,
Flying in the shape of a "v".

Joelle U. lives in Roaring Branch,PA. She wrote Winter Is On Its Way because winter is her favorite time of the year. Joelle's favorite part of her piece is "Apples are atop the ground, Except for the breeze you cannot hear a sound."

Home
By Margaret B.

A ceiling,
4 walls,
And a floor,
Holding a family,
     -Is not just a home.

Home is where we've cried, is where we have laughed, where we have hoped, where we have learned, where we have grown, and where we have lived life. Home is like a blanket -a sanctuary from the outside world -almost like a shield. Home keeps you from the darkness and the evil. Home is a place to let it all out, to let your true inner self shine.

Home is anywhere you want it to be -it doesn't just have to be walls, home is anywhere that gives you the feeling of safety and love, happiness and joy.

Margaret B. writes, "When I turned eleven I realized that the outside world can be mean and critical. I am so grateful that my home is my blanket from the outside world. My favorite sentence is: 'Home is like a blanket - a sanctuary from the outside world - almost like a shield.'"

The Heart of a Forest
By Alana C.

Through the woods the birdsong flies,
Into the endless bright blue skies.
Carrying stories of people and places,
As the beauty of spring breaks free from its cases.
The flowers will bloom, all colors and shapes,
While towering trees shade the forest like drapes.
Then the vivid colors will fade into green,
As the beginning of summer now is seen.
The bright sun burns the crispy, soft, leaves,
While all animals settle in, along with the bees.
Soon the leaves will fall, spinning down to the ground,
Whisping and twirling through the air all around.
The mountains are splattered with orange, yellow, and red,
As the animals curl up, cozy, warm, and fed.
Then the forest is bare, not a sound to be heard,
While the bitter morning frost into its den is lured.
Snowflakes start falling, each different in a way,
So many, so many, coming down all day.
The forest is blanketed in a silver, gleaming white,
While the birdsong is silent each day followed by night.
But spring will arrive again in just a short time,
When all creatures have peace, and the forest comes alive.

Until The Gas Wells Came
By Alexis P.

Until the gas wells came

Our fields were full of flowers

That seemed to have magical powers

We loved to run and jump

We were never just a lump

Until the gas wells came

We had a lot of fun

Yes, fun in the sun

We would do anything to get that back

But that's something we all lack

Until the gas wells came

(untitled)
By Kathryne R.

Summer
hot sticky
swim run sweat
pool air conditioner ice wood stove
slip freeze shiver
cold frosty
winter

Kathryne R. chose this topic because she likes both summer and winter. She thinks they are both times to enjoy and their weather is very different. Kathryne's favorite lines are the ones about winter and how cold it is.

My Christmas Home
By Darby K.

I woke up and all I saw was high chain link fences. Underneath me was a soft squishy bed. The last thing I remembered was being thrown out the window of a big man's car. I was very sore from hitting the pavement. Over the next few days I slowly began to look more like a regular puppy. I got over ring worm and my black fluffy coat came back. I was fed a lot so I got some meat on my bones. I was glad that I was no longer living with people who mistreated me, but I was also very sad. All day I lay on my bed alone in the cage. It was two days before Christmas and it looked like I would spend the holiday in the cold shelter.

As closing time neared, a woman came running in through the front door of the shelter. She was a chubby lady with brown hair. She told the lady at the front desk that her name was Stacey and she was looking for a puppy for her daughter for Christmas. The adoption specialist walked her down the rows of puppies, telling Stacey a little bit about each one. When they reached my cage the specialist began to tell Stacey about my history. Stacey interrupted her immediately and exclaimed "This is the one!" I guess you could say I was cute. I had big floppy ears and a really long tail. I was mostly black with white on my belly, a strip of white down my nose and the tip of my tail. But being part Saint Bernard and part

Black Labrador, I would grow to be an enormous, extremely hyper dog.

That night Stacey took me home with her. She hid me in the garage and told me that I had to wait until Christmas morning to meet her daughter Sarah. For those two days I sat alone in the garage just like I did at the shelter. I got so bored that I took to chewing on the wood boards along the floor. I was happy to be out of the shelter but I was still lonely.

I wanted someone to play with me and take me on long walks through the woods. I wondered if I would ever have a place to call home. On Christmas Eve Stacey came and silently took me into her large, immaculate home. She tied a big red bow around my neck and placed me underneath the Christmas tree. When Stacey went to bed I lay on my back gazing dreamily at the shiny silver and red balls dangling of the tree. They looked so tempting but I contained myself. I didn't want to lose this chance at a good home.

Just as the sun was rising, I was woken by a young girl in plaid pajamas with frizzy brown hair screaming. She picked me up and hugged me so tight I could barely breathe. She told me all about how we would be best friends and we would do everything together. We all ate a huge breakfast of pancakes and bacon. Then she took me outside to have a snowball fight and we went for a long walk on the trail through the woods surrounding the farm house. Afterwards we came inside and snuggled around the fire. I had some presents from a few people and they let me rip up the wrapping paper. I got so many toys and Sarah spent all day playing with me. I knew then that I had found my home.

The inspiration to write about the adopted dog came from Darby recieving a puppy from the SPCA last

Christmas and thinking it would make a good story. Darby's favorite part is when Sarah gets the puppy on Christmas morning.

Lena's Diary: A Sense of Place
By Sarah H.

December 8th:

I've never really had a "Sense of Place." The thought of it can be divided a thousand different ways, but to me it's just two; either you have it or you don't. For me, it's definitely the second, especially since my mom just informed me that my dad's business firm would be relocating-AGAIN-for the fifth time in the past eight years! I started writing in this diary because it makes me feel like *someone* is listening. To further my disconnection with "place," it is pretty much nonexistent at home too, since my mom is always at the ER (she's a doctor there) and my dad's business just keeps growing . . . so he's never home either!!!

December 10th:

I stopped caring after the third time we moved and trying to make friends. I stopped joining sports and clubs, and I stopped riding my bike to local "hang-out spots" to socialize with kids my age. To me it wasn't really worth it, because I knew that I'd be moving again soom. Somehow, my mom fit in just fine in every place we went . . . she always got a new job at the local hospital, and her coworkers would invite her to their churches for services, or out for a day of shopping with the girls.

January 23rd:

My first day of school in Carson City, Nevada actually wasn't terrible. A few girls invited me to their lunch table, which has never happened before, and everyone there was very kind! There were boys there too, and it was a little weird having some boys stare at me a little more than necessary. I did spend a little more time in front of the mirror today in effort to make a good first impression, and I wore a bit more perfume and mascara. One boy paid special attention to me!!!

P.S.-His name is Nate!!!!

February 7th:

Nate and I are actually friends!!!! In the past few weeks, I've learned that Nate's a senior, has five younger siblings, and volunteers at the local zoo. I think this place might be different than anywhere else I've lived. I have a feeling that something unexpected is about to happen . . .

February 14th:

My day was INCREDIBLE!! Today's my birthday, and I didn't want any special attention, so I never told anyone. During sociology, I looked out the window to the amazing view or campus, and I noticed a huge, colorful banner spread out on the grass. Looking closer, I read: "Happy Birthday Lena!!" I stared at it in awe. Behind me Nate's voice said, "Do you like it?" I spun around and said, "You did this?" His smile answered me, and then he sat a nicely wrapped gift in front of me. I carefully opened it, and when I saw what it was I gasped. It was a very antique looking book with a shiny mirror cover and entitled; "How and Where to Find Your Sense of Place." The directions told me I was to read the book every night before bed, and follow every instruction. When I looked up, I saw that Nate was gone, but a note was left on his desk, written in his familiar handwriting. He said that I was very special to him, and that's why he wanted me to find my "Sense of Place," in hopes that I'd stay.

March 1st:

I'm crying as I write this because of all of the unbelievable things that have happened to me recently. I followed the directions in the book, and every night after falling asleep, I would travel to wonderful places in my dreams. I visited Antarctica, Paris, Hawaii, the Bahamas and more. I had a sense of place!! I was with my family and friends, and they weren't busy with work or commitments!! I felt like I belonged and it was the most amazing feeling ever! The books' directions were listed after the prompt: "I don't have a Sense of Place because ...." I chose the option "We move all of the time," It seemed like it was there just for me. On page 77, the rules were as follows;

1. Believe in yourself
2. Make friends (see rule number 1 to help here) they will help you get through this.
3. Talk to your parents (tell them how you feel)
4. After you do these things, look at the front cover of this book. If you see a smile there, then you have found YOUR Sense of Place. Congratulations!!

Sarah H. is a 7th grader at Mansfield Jr./Sr. High School. She enjoys playing soccer and basketball and spending time with her family. Sarah writes "even though I'm nothing like the character that I wrote about, I enjoy writing using another person's point of view. My favorite part was when Lena looked at the front cover, and since she saw a smile, she knew that her sense of place had been found."

Adventures in the Woods
By Jared S.

My dad and I walk quietly down the narrow path. It's quiet. I hear the leaves crunching beneath my boot. I can see nothing, as it's pitch black, but no worry, the sun will rise soon. We are almost to our destination. The sun is rising we just get to the blind.

I can now see the scenery, the sight is beautiful, the leaves are falling from all different directions, not one the same. I can clearly see the crick rapidly running below me. The sight of gracious deer prancing in the field not one big enough to shoot. The sight of my green and white arrow with the razor sharp broadhead sitting gently on my bow.

The sound of squirrels playing. The acorns falling from the tree way above. The wind whistling from tree to tree and back again. The smell is crisp but fresh like the smell of a morning breeze. The smell of the dirt from the bare ground. The smell of the dead leaves floating through the air like powder in front of a fan.

The taste of dirt in your mouth like week old milk. As I sit there excitedly waiting for the deer to come is good but when a deer comes and it's big enough to shoot your heart is beating out of your chest it gets harder to breathe. All that excitement is built up like kettle corn in a pot and you put all of that energy into power and draw the heavy bow back and the whole world slows down. You can concentrate on the target and pull the release. The arrow goes flying and you see that it hits the deer in the arteries. We now wait for the deer to die and then track the blood trail.

We now then climb out of the tree stand and follow the blood trail and I am bouncing off the wall of excitement, then I get serious. We have to follow the blood trail. We come to the end and there is the deer, now we can get excited again. All our hard work has paid off. As we drag it out, I think to myself, I am very lucky.

Slave on the Run
By Molly C.

"Wake up Katherine," my Ma softly, but urgently said.

I sleepily blinked my eyes open to a dully burning kerosene lamp. I suddenly remembered, tonight was the night we stowaway! I rolled out of the straw bedding making sure not to wake any of the others.

"Hurry," Ma silently urged with her hands.

I slid my work clothes over my worn down pajamas and touched the soft, woven, leather necklace hidden discretely under my clothes.

"I'm ready," I nodded and we silently slid out of the mud hut that I had known as home forever. We silently stole through the night and I thought of what my Pa had told me many sunrises ago. "Follow the Drinking Gourd (a pattern of stars familiar to many African slaves) for it will show you the way." I wish he could have come with us.

I am an only child and was very lucky. My family, Mama, Papa, and me we're sold as a pack, so we all went to the same farm, the Botashry Farm. It pains me to think about that prison, that torture chamber of a farm. My Ma and I were lucky. We worked in the house cooking and cleaning. My Pa was not so lucky. He had to work in the fields with back breaking work, sun beating harshly on his body like a never ending whip. He worked from dawn until dusk and was always bone tired as he came home to our little mud hut. Out in the fields, the overseers did not care if a slave worked to death, slaves were cheap. If one died they would just go to a slave market and buy another one. Pa was one of those slaves. He worked until one day he snapped and life was never fully restored again. Before he died, he gave me this woven leather necklace with a polished stone that had been smoothed by the sands of blue African sea and said, "You take care of that now Katherine darling, it's been in our family forever, and I don't want it getting lost now you understand?" I nodded, and my hand touched his forehead as he took his last weak breath. 1 touched the woven necklace around my neck and snapped back to reality.

"Come on Katherine, you're draggin' your feet now, pick it up!" I hurriedly ran to catch up. The sun was starting to rise again. "Mama, when are we going to stop?"

"Soon baby soon," she replied.

Not long after, we arrived at our first safe house. It had a freedom quilt hanging outside on the porch giving us a sign it was safe. We tapped on the door and a pudgy woman with a flour streaked apron took one look at our chocolate brown skin, greeted us, and rushed us inside. She showed us our rooms, which were cleverly hidden behind cabinets.

"I urge you to be quiet," the woman kindly but sternly said as she pushed the cabinets back in place. She said that she would wake us when the stars of the Drinking Gourd aligned with the moon. With that she slid the cabinets back into place leaving us completely hidden. She came and woke us exactly when the last star scurried into place. We traveled to many more safe houses on our path to freedom and never once were caught by bounty hunters. As we neared our last safe house before freedom I listened to the familiar humming of the crickets and screeching of the owls and thought to myself, "We made it!" We really did. I began to weep tears of happiness. My Mama hugged me and started to cry too, as if she knew what I was thinking. As we made the last rap tap tap on the door I thought to myself, we will never again see the blood upon our backs but I will forever feel like a slave on the run.

Molly C. was inspired by a fifth grade field trip to Gettysburg where she learned about the Underground Railroad. Molly is a seventh grade student at Mansfield Jr./Sr. High School. She enjoys cross country, swimming, and being active. Molly also enjoys reading and spending time with her family.

Janie's Better Days
By Dannielle K.

"What's ADHD?" I whispered to the short, plump, guidance counselor the last ten minutes of the school day.

"Well, ADHD is a disorder. . ." she began, launching into a daylong speech about how people with ADHD couldn't focus well. It sort of made sense, because, lately, my peers had started calling me "ADHD girl". I had known for a while I had less than the attention span of a goldfish, I just didn't know there was an official name for it. I like goldfish.

I half listened to her talk; half let my eyes flick around to different objects. A crawling fly, the hugest bird I had ever seen, (I think it was a bloated robin) landing in of the apple tree outside, and the bustle of the students at their lockers as the final bell rang.

"Is that enough information?" she asked. "Maybe you would like some pamphlets."

As she turned to look, I kinda did a little potty dance (I didn't need to go). She handed me the pamphlets, I thanked her, and dashed to my bus for the three second bus ride to the hotel I lived in. See, when my Dad went to fight in Iraq, the bank took our house, so Mom and I moved to Mansfield, Pennsylvania. I was told there were a lot of gas drills here. Mom got a job as a maid in this hotel.

Mom tells me not to watch TV, because paying for the cable bill comes out of her paycheck. Which, come to think of it, is probably why I have nothing to say when anyone talks about MTV, which is all the time. Instead, I grab a packet of Scooby-Doo gummies and head for the basement laundry room to see if Mom needs any laundry delivered.

The next day at school, there's a new girl named Logan. I always sit alone at lunch, so maybe she'll sit with me.

When I walk into the cafeteria with my packed lunch of roast beef and fruit snacks, I scream so loud when I realize what she's reading, the whole world can hear me. She happens to be reading *Girl in Blue* by Ann Rinaldi. I was reading the same exact book (Ann Rinaldi is my favorite author) last week, except it was so tattered and torn it could have been printed during the Civil War, which is when it takes place.

"That's the best book I've ever read!" I yell, earning some dirty looks from the lunch monitors. We talk about books for a while, until she says, "when my mom homeschooled me, she had me read a lot of historic fiction."

"Really?" I ask, "I always wanted to be homeschooled."

"Maybe I could see if my mom would homeschool you."

I didn't want to hurt my friend to the point she'd never talk to me again, but, I also didn't want to hurt my mom's checkbook, because I wasn't sure how much it would cost. "That's okay. I'm not sure how much longer we'll be in this area anyway."

That's when I tell her why we're in Mansfield, about how my dad was in Iraq. How my family was so poor, we had to sell our car a couple of weeks ago, how my mom was a maid in the hotel we lived in. When I finished, she stared at me, stunned. "I-I'm so sorry," she stammered, her eyes tearing up, "My uncle, he was in Afghanistan. He was in there for about a month. He was fighting, and he's been missing ever since."

Now it's my turn to be stunned. Not so much for Logan's uncle, but mostly for dad. I thought he'd either be alive or not when he came home. I didn't think we would have to wonder.

I'm about to ask her how long he's been missing, when she gets up from the table and runs out of the cafeteria. I want to go follow her, but I've already gotten in trouble for yelling and just hope this doesn't ruin our friendship.

I eat the rest of my lunch in a guilty silence, arguing with myself.

"You shouldn't have brought up a sensitive subject that with someone you just met."

"How was I supposed to know her uncle was MIA?"

When I get home, I' m surprised to see my mom sitting on her bed, let alone on the phone. She gives it to me and I hear, "Janie, I'm coming home."

Dannielle K. writes "I wrote Janie's Better Days because Mansfield and the surrounding areas have many gas wells. There are also a lot of people that don't have a job, and many families are very poor. Furthermore, brave soldiers are overseas serving our country. My favorite part is when Janie's father is coming home."

(untitled)
By Megan C.

Dear Jessica,

Texas is Mars. A barren land that has nothing to offer. A thief that has stolen my best friend. Texas, it has tumbleweed here or there, but nothing much. Without you life is without color. How is Texas by the way? Do you wish that your old friends are there with you? Do you wish that you were back in Pennsylvania? I sure wish that you were here, but that outlaw of a state, Texas, stole you from me.

I guess that even thousands of miles can't break apart this friendship. Whenever a new student comes to school I've never thought about the friends that they are leaving behind. Until now. Either the next town over or all the way across the country there is a best friend that misses them terribly.

Texas is just a place with lots of cowboys and dirt. Why would anyone want to live on Mars, when earth is right here? Just like Mars, Texas is just a barren piece of land. I can see Texas now, with his scruffy hair, cowboy hat, and dust-caked boots. Just a thief, waiting and watching for someone to claim as his own. Why has Texas stolen you from me?

Megan C. writes, "I'm thirteen years old and I've been friends with my best friend Jessica for about six years, but on May 20th she moved because her father accepted a job in Texas. That's a long way from Pennsylvania where I live. When she told me that she was going to move to Texas I thought about all of the things that we wouldn't be able to do anymore. Like taking walks, jumping on her trampoline, going swimming, and much more. So when my Reading teacher told me that the subject for the contest was

"A Sense of Place," I instantly thought about Jessica in Texas. I've never been to Texas before so I tried to imagine what I think it looks like. All of the other possible topics seemed to disappear. My favorite sentence of my work is "Whether they move to the next town over or across the country you're sure to find a best friend that misses them terribly."

My Place
By Alison H.

In an empty gym I lace my basketball shoes
and take a quick glance at the banners of names.
Names of people who led MHS to great victories;
people who shot at the same foul line dripping
sweat.
I take a second glance and imagine my name on
one
I hear the whispers of the trophies telling me you
can be on one.
I listen to the squeaks of my shoes on the gym floor
where Tom McMullen played
I think about him shooting in the same gym,
Accomplishing greatness.

Swoosh!
Another ball goes through the net.
I take a deep breath.
I feel like anything is possible.
I feel as if I can do so many great things in here,
But it has been a long stay here.
I must go.
I must leave my sense of place.

Reviving Me
By Sara W.

"I hate you! Can't you just understand me?!" I hurl the words back at my parents, gladly throwing them like stones. Thunder rumbles over my head, an agreement or a warning. I don't care. I can't take this anymore. I storm down the driveway, just walking away from them, not forever, just long enough to build my tolerance, again. Raindrops patter on my head and I shake them off, and then ignore it when a torrent of rain attempts to wash me away. I guess no one cares today. Tears start to mix with the rain and I let them flow, choking sobs rattle me, and there's no stopping me today. I close my eyes and lift my face as wind brushes my cropped hair and breathe deeply, just as a car swerves off the road and crushes me. I don't feel, see or hear it; I just sense it and open my eyes to look down on a bloody pavement with a mangled body that has my face and curled black hair tangled around it. "Crap ..." I mutter and everything goes black.

I'm floating almost, and there are no scents or colors or feels to it, just a gentle thrumming sound and the vast emptiness. I try to breathe deeply and process what happened, and in the back of my head a little cord seems to pull me. I see or, I guess, feel myself being carried into a hospital and doctors cutting away my clothes and staunching many blood wounds. There is yelling and orderly panic as a short, kind nurse feels a faint pulse at my neck and smooths ratted hair from my face. She promptly winces when she finds a long shard of glass imbedded in my ear that slits open my scalp. Against my better judgment, I scream, and rub my eyes to banish the image. Again I look around and search for anything in the darkness.

Then I see it, a flash of dancing light ahead. I stare at it, hardly believing, when from it a delighted scream of laughter echoes. I stop breathing; it's my best friend Charlotte and I, when we were about five years old, just before she was in a horrible accident when a bridge collapsed and her and her family plunged off a cliff. It's like I see us inside me as we run around her yard, hunting for bugs. I'm on the verge of reaching out and joining them when I hear a blood curdling scream behind me. It winds up into a wind that blows up behind me and flushes away the happiness exploding inside me. "No!" I choke out as smoke fills my lungs. I cough and see the last fading yellow streak explode into and angry blazing fire, the one that wiped out half the town and almost killed me when I was twelve. I can't stop the rapidly rushing death, so I curl up, matching the little girl that's me in the corner of the hissing inferno that I see in my mind's eye. I remember how my tears evaporated on my cheeks as the building caves, and a fireman reaches in and scooped twelve year old me out into the street. He leaves current me though and I cough painfully as the smoke clogs my lungs. White light explodes and I'm standing on the side of a neighborhood street looking down at my bloody mangled body, seeing the blank eyes roll up to meet mine and a raspy voice echo through it.

"You were saved too much. Die or appreciate what you have unrightfully been given over and over." I could only stare as the mouth widens and noise crashes into me, rocking me back into silence, a horrible stony silence with nothing but ungrateful me. I realize how close I came to death so many times, when I waved to Charlotte in her car when I decided last minute to stay behind, when I was saved from the fire and countless other times that are now obviously warnings to appreciate my place in this world. Tears run as I cry for my poor parents, so much that the darkness ebbs away and I find them standing over me in a hospital bed. I lick my cracked lips and whisper much needed words. "I'm sorry..." loading everything into those words and almost laughing when my parents both embrace me. I sigh in relief and settle into this sense of place.

Sara W. loves being creative. Her topic was inspired from the components of her favorite places like certain smells, colors, and sounds. Sara's favorite line is "Not forever, just long enough to build up my tolerance," because when she's mad, time alone helps her to feel better.

The Jungle
By Dawson H.

I'm in a jungle of music.
The bass is surrounding me like rain and it's
soaking me.
My bed is a raft, floating through the river.
The singer's voice is like a call from the wild.
The guitar is the rush of the water.
As the parts piece together, I get enveloped in its
grasp.
I fall out of the raft and all my senses are gone.
I'm disoriented and frantic, but the music calms
me. As my senses come back, I realize I'm no longer
in the jungle.
I see nothing but colors.
Shades of blues, greens, and purples exploding in
front of me.
The colors are changing with the rhythm of the
music. The blues change to reds, the greens change
to oranges, and the purples change to blacks.
It scares me, but it's almost calming in a way.
It completes me.

Dawson H. chose to write about music because music is his passion and life. In his writing piece, he explained the world music took him to. His favorite part of the work was the entire last paragraph. It took music to a colorful perspective, capturing an image in the readers' minds.

The Octagon
By Anthony W.

The octagon is an important place. It is a place in the woods. It's a place that's in the heart of the golden rods. The octagon is what I hunt in.

Last year I shot a ten point with a drop tine out of the octagon. The octagon is shaped as an octagon with eight sides. It has recliners and windows. The octagon has a valley to the right of it and the rest of the land is flat. This has many animals, such as deer, squirrel, bear, and turkey. I hunt this place every year. My favorite spot to look at while I'm hunting is the row of pine trees. That is where I usually spot the first animal.

If the octagon changed, that wouldn't be good. That's the part of land where I hunt, fish, hangout, and listen to nature. I wouldn't be able to do those things if it changed.

This is my favorite place to be. I love the octagon. You'll love the octagon too. If it changes I would be sad. I don't think it is going to change. It is on a two hundred acre plus, on private land. When I grow up I'm going to own the octagon.

Anthony W. is 13 years old and an eighth grader at Williamson Jr/Sr high school. In his spare time Anthony likes to hunt, fish, and play sports. Anthony has played soccer, baseball, football, and wrestled. He has also raced go-karts. Anthony chose to write about hunting because it is an enjoyable hobby of his.

What Will I Do Now?
By Kathryn B.

I looked around my now empty room. What had once been filled with pictures and postcards and posters from various places, now looked so lifeless with only the white walls staring back at me.

I was born into a gas company family. I never got very attached to things like a view out a window because I knew sooner or later; it would only be a distant memory.

There really was *no place* that I belonged. The only thing that I knew how to be a part of was the gas company my dad worked for.

My older brother, Mark, walked into the room and sighed. The two of us were best friends. I told him everything and he told me everything.

"Mom said we're leaving in five." He said and grabbed one of the last few boxes still in my room.

"I'll be right out." I picked one of the other boxes and stacked it on top of the other one he had and carried the last one down stairs after him.

We walked out the front door and loaded the last boxes in our U-Haul. Mark turned around and got in his car. I followed him and took shotgun.

"Are you ready for a chance at a new life and a fresh start?" I took mom's line. She would have to get over it.

"As I'll ever be." He said and started the car.

"Maybe we'll stay there this time. Long enough to belong."

Mark just scoffed at me and sent me a sad smile. "You have high hopes ... "

I gazed out my window and absentmindedly twisted my brown hair.

A few miles passed before either one of us said anything.

"Dru, you know that I hope things work out here, right?" Mark asked me. I sighed and gazed back out the window. "yeah.... I know. You just don't seem too optimistic."

Now it was Mark's turn to sigh. We settled back into our silence.

"Mark ... " I said at the same time my phone rang. I gave him the universal "Hold on" gesture and answered.

Mom was on the other end.

"Dru! We're going to stop at the gas station. Your dad is hungry. I'm sure you can go ahead of us." Mom told us.

"Alright," I said and hit the end button. 1 threw my phone up on the dash.

"Like I was saying, I'm sorry that I don't understand why this isn't important to you. But I need somewhere to belong." I tried. I wanted, no *needed,* to get my point across.

Mark took a deep breath before beginning, "I know. And I'm sorry." We drove on in silence.

The car jerked forward and we spun on some black ice. Mark's head hit the steering wheel and I heard a scream, not realizing until later that it was my own.

I frantically searched for my phone. I dialed 911.

"911, what's your emergency?" Came the operator's voice.

"Some jackass just rear-ended us and we hit some black ice and my brother hit his head on the steering wheel and he won't wake up'" I was bawling now while I told her my location. She stayed on the line while I waited for the emergency vehicles.

I hung up after a sobbed, "Thank you." when the ambulance and cops got here.

I told them the same story that I told the operator and watched as they loaded my brother on the stretcher. I called my mom and it went to voicemail.

"Come to the hospital." I said flatly and climbed in the back of the ambulance.

Mark stirred, groaned, and was out again.

Mom was at the hospital when we got there. She wrapped her arms around me. "None of this is your fault." She promised me.

I gave dad a sad smile. We sat down with me in the middle on one of the not so comfortable waiting room couches. We idly chatted.

A few hours later, when dad was at a vending machine, a throat cleared near us. There was a doctor with a sad look on his face.

"I'm so sorry," was all that I heard before everything spiraled in and out of focus. I was too shocked to cry. I lost my best friend. My brother. Who will I talk to when mom and dad get on my nerves? He was my familiar thing wherever we went. Now, I *really* had nowhere to belong.

My Place
By Amanda T.

When I first received the Endless Mountain Writing Project pamphlet by my 8th grade science teacher, Mr. Perry, and read the subject "A Sense of Place", I will admit the first thought that popped into my head was *this will be easy. I can do this with no problem.* Then, again, I got the pamphlet in the mail and the same thought crossed my mind, but I was mistaken.

My original thought was that I could write a romantic love story about how the guy and girl meet at a certain spot, fall in love, get in a fight, realize that they can't live without each other, return to the same spot only to find their significant other waiting for them, and ride off into the sunset to live happily ever after. Just like in the fairytales. I figured I could wrap that story up in a couple days. One week later, I had nothing.

On my next effort I got a few paragraphs completed, only to find that I couldn't bring myself to finish the story. It just felt all wrong, so I wiped the slate clean and started fresh. For this next story, I gritted my teeth and pushed myself to finish it, and I did it! I had planned to turn that story in, until I read it over a day or two later. It *still* felt wrong. Something wasn't right, and I had no idea what it was! The next week was just a bunch of useless attempts to find the best story.

It wasn't until a conversation with Mr. Perry that I got it. I was explaining to him my frustration when he suggested that I write about that fact that I *didn't* have a place. To be honest, I didn't agree with him at first. I had a place! In fact, I had many places, yet his words gnawed at me like mosquitos on a hot summer day that whole day and even into that night. Nevertheless, here I sit writing this because I had come to realize he was, in reality, correct.

Let me point out that I was right too. Of course I have places: my house, my clique, my church, my family. I have come to the conclusion that just because I have places, doesn't mean that I have a *sense of place*. I know there is a difference, yet I can't put my finger on what it is. As I was saying though, Mr. Perry had a point. If I couldn't bring myself to complete a story successfully about a sense of place, should I take that as a sign that I don't have one?

My parents decided to participate in this year's writing contest too, and when they gave me theirs to read, they had excellent stories! More importantly, though, they had a something to write about. They *had* a sense of place. Even my best friend had something to write about, and all I had was about a billion ideas that I couldn't complete.

In the end, it makes me wonder what will happen in the future. Will I ever find a sense of place? Can I ever find something like my parents found? Do I even have a sense of place? If so, where is my place? Will I ever be able to find it?

This brings me to the end of my journey, after countless hours of headaches and a trash can full with crumpled up papers, I finally had something to write about. More notably, it felt right. It didn't feel like any of those fairytales I was struggling to write. All and all, I came to realize that I don't have a sense of place and maybe I will never, but no matter what, I need make the most of it because ultimately, that's what matters.

Amanda T. writes "My favorite piece in this story is definitely the part about is when I am describing my original thought about the girl and guy who ride of in the sunset like in the fairy tales."

Thinking Ahead
By Anna M.

The class clown is cracking jokes
And the teacher is holding back a smile
I lean back in my chair
And think ahead awhile

I wonder what we'll be thinking
As we walk across the stage
13 years for a handshake
Seems like such a waste

Some will wonder how they made it
Some will ask themselves what's next
Some will barely cry a tear
Some will be a wreck

But what we'll gain while we're here
Can never be replaced
And we'll walk out of this school
With a smile on our face

We'll make a million memories
And find some lifelong friends
And the more we think about it
We won't want to see the end

Of course we're only Freshmen
We still have more to do
I stand and gather my books
and go to period two.

(untitled)
By Maggie B.

A put-put-putting sound filled the sun-burnt, freckled farmers' children's ears as they rode down the country roads in the back of their father's mud-splattered silver pickup truck. The sun seemed to make the cattails glitter and the tips of the straw looked as though they were spun from gold. Leaves and weeds swayed with the breeze of fresh air. Dust and dirt clouded the road as they drove forward. They coughed as the truck slowly stopped at the family's pasture. Simultaneously, the family of three hopped onto the dried out mud.

Little Silas and Flora smiled as they walked up the dirt path to the pond. This was a tradition they had always done with their father. Watching the sunset on the summer solstice brought joyful memories to the small family. Much to their dismay, this would turn out to be the last time they watched the golden rays fade away into the dark curtain of night sitting by the edge of the pond. By summer solstice next year, their special place would be replaced with bright fluorescent lights and high fences with towers protruding atop the fences.

School was now in session for the two kids. Their father continued to run the family farm in the meantime. He watched the hills with a toughened face; the future was undeniable now. As calendar pages flipped and seasons transitioned from one to another, foreign metal structures disturbed the scenic mountainside of fall foliage, Truck after truck snaked through the winding roads. Bright lights illuminated the night sky before Christmas making it impossible to sleep,

Alas, after a near fatal accident in the road, Silas's and Flora's father explained what the world they knew was changing to, No more would it be a peaceful haven in which only they lived in. Their world was transforming into one that they had to share with strangers-and these strangers had different styles and talked unlike anybody they had known before. Being youthful, the children hadn't been exposed to such things. They didn't understand why they had to stay on the property; they never had before.

However, life goes on. Mountainside Farm was still their home, even if they had to share a little bit of it now, The year was chipped away and as was the road. If the potholes were bad before, then they were now crater-holes. Road construction was county-wide and constant. Going to school took the children about twenty minutes before everything had happened. Now it took them forty minutes,

At last, the school year had finished, Silas and Flora left a little bit wiser and a little less sheltered. Life at school had even changed. Exposure to kids from outside of the county allowed them to pick up different habits-good and bad-and encouraged them to see past differences, though conformity still existed. Reflectively, they let the bus doors close behind them as they raced to the front door.

Tenseness lingered in the atmosphere. Curiously, they parted ways in search of their father, but he was not inside. Flora ran out the screen door letting it slam behind her. The family's dog, Jack, chased after her in a concerned manner. She found Mr. Harrison in the barn with her father. Hearing an agitated conversation she backed away and eavesdropped,

"I'm sorry Mr. Taylors, but I just don't see why you won't lease your rights to the company. It's foolish nonsense if you ask me." Mr. Harrison stated haughtily. "Well I didn't ask you, now did I?" retorted Flora's father. Mr. Harrison leaned against the rusty colored boards and spat.

"Just a friendly suggestion is all. There's no need to get all worked up over it. I just don't understand your ideals."

"Thanks, but no thanks. My ideals are idealistic for my family. I don't want to see my kids grow up unsafe in their own home. This is my property; I'll do what I want. Now if you don't mind, I need to fix my kids some dinner. Goodnight, Mr. Harrison."

Mr. Harrison was silent as he raised his hand in leave-taking as he sauntered down the dirt road to his truck. Mr. Taylors shook his head in dismay as he watched his neighbor give in to greed. Giving one final glance to Mr. Harrison, Flora's father tapped her on her shoulder and they walked inside their home together. Home was the exact word for it. Home was the only place they had ever known, it was their place.

Maggie B writes "I wrote about the Natural Gas Industry because that's what's happening now. That's what our place in Bradford County revolves around right now. My favorite part of the work, particularly, is the incorporation and description of the changing scenery throughout the piece."

Vintage Memories
By Anna C.

She sits on the attic floor
Opening up a dusty old trunk,
Pulling back the packing
That was keeping the treasures safe.

Inside lies a dress,
Turning yellow with age.
She will need to have it cleaned and fitted,
If she is to wear it for that special day.
The dress is fairly old,
With hand-sewn beads and lace,
But she has known it is the one for her
Since she was a just a tot.
Lying by the dress' side,
A stack of old photographs
Crinkled and weathered with age.
Photographs from a time long ago.

She carefully pulls out the stack,
Delicately holding the top picture up
Her eyes begin to tear,
For in the picture is her mother,
Wearing that very dress.

Her grandmother shuffles up behind her.
And with love and sadness in her voice,
Tells her granddaughter
How much this would have meant to her mother.
For she passed
Just after the girl was born,
And with the father gone already
Only the grandmother was left to care for the child.

The grandmother gingerly picks up
Another photograph from the stack.
This one of a little girl
Playing dress up in a beaded and laced wedding
gown.

As the tears begin to flow
From each woman's face,
They share memories
From the past.

Of a time when all the little girl wanted
Was to grow up and get married,
In the very same dress
That her mother married her father.

She carefully puts the photographs
Back in the trunk,
Bringing out the dress
For the approaching day.

She gently closes the lid
And takes to the stairs after her grandmother,
Being sure to shut off the light,
So the trunk can wait for another little girl.

She will find its treasures,
And hopefully add to the bunch.
Continuing the cycle
Of its vintage memories

Anna C. writes "When choosing a poem topic, anything can inspire me, whether it be a word or picture. Vintage Memories was born when I was reading and the word "vintage" was in the text, something just clicked and I began to write and a fairly short time later I had a poem. I would have to say the fourth stanza is my favorite. I feel it gives you a clear image of a young lady kneeling down seeing that one special gown and pictures that represent both her history and future. Her history is shown in the fact that the photographs are of family and the dress she will be wearing, yet the future is shown by the happy couples in the pictures and she would be able to picture how she will look as a bride."

Change Through the Years
By Courtney G.

Days and nights come and go
Like spirits through the years
The land continues to change
And people's faces disappear

What started out as a natural place is soon
succumbed to man
The trees are cleared one by one
And houses dominated the land
Children run together, shouting and laughing in
play
A new world to see
A new time has come
As well as another day

Soon the houses are built higher
And wood paths turned to man made roads
People come, of all race and religion
Seeking freedom and a place to call their own
One house turns into two and more businesses
appear
The town is gone
The city has come
Bring people from far and near
History has been made
As another day comes
But will not stay

More people come
By boats and by trains
Looking for work and a place to stay
They go to the factories
They go to the mines

They don't know what will come of tomorrow
But they know it what will matter in time
Building their empire higher
Making it all they intend
They work towards the future
As another day is brought to its end

The cities keep growing
People keep coming
And life goes forward with time
Women are working
And times are changing
Changing for your future and for mine

You can't redo a day that's already gone by
There's no way to turn back the clock
The same day will never come again
The world will always change
Nothing can ever stay the same
But the sense that this place is home will never go
away

This is where I belong
By Abby S.

The leaves are beginning to change now. It looks so beautiful at the lake, especially at this time of year. There are apple trees lined along the edges. Fresh apples are hanging on the trees now and little ones are starting to fall from them. They're all so ripe, even the ones on the ground aren't rotten. If I could I would be swimming right now. But the lake is too cold during fall. If only. I've loved the water for as long as I can remember. My favorite is when you sit on the bottom, and look straight up. You can see everything, everything, from there. There's just no view like it. The red leaves dance on top of the water like they're angry flames, while the green ones are trying to calm them down. It's gorgeous. This is where I belong. Out in the wilderness enjoying the view, just like my ancestors, and all the other people that came to this beautiful country.

Abby S. is a sophomore at Athens Area High School. She likes to write and likes being able to express herself. Abby is also a member of her school's track team and Student Council. The inspiration for this story came from the orchard that Abby's grandfather and his family owned in Pennsylvania. She writes "I wrote this story because it's one of the most amazing views ever, and no one can bother you. It's one of those places where you feel like you do belong there, and that's where you're supposed to be." Abby's favorite line is "The red leaves dance on the top of the water like they're angry flames, while the green ones are trying to calm them down. "

(untitled)
By Wade P.

"Nope don't load em son; they've still gotta be cut in half to get the short steel price!" This was a phrase I was used to hearing. In fact it was one of many I would hear throughout the day at the yard.

"Here you can start sortin' this pile; make sure you cut off all the brass from the copper tubing and keep em in a separate barrel." "I don't want no wastin'a that copper either it's up fifty cents a pound this month from last and we can't have any goin' as brass weight."

I take these words with a grain of salt as our "payday" depends solely on the efficiency and attention paid to how we chop, sort, and load the metals. Not to mention salt. It's the middle of July and the sun is not merciful in its attempts to bake us all in its eighty-five degree weather. We can just stand still and the sweat trickles down our face and back.

"I think if we keep goin' at this rate we'll have a load strapped down to take to the mill before closin' time," my father says with a tired smile.

I smile back in recognition of his optimism. It gives me immense pride to see my father look at our hard work with such enthusiasm. We pause for only a moment and back to our job we go, back to the "oven."

"Do ya think mosta these vans will have catalytic convertors in em?" I refer to the halfdozen or so rotted-out van bodies that appear to be only held together by the remnants of their former factory paint jobs, which now seem to complimenting the orange rust that grows around their fenders.

"I don't know buddy," he says with slight hesitation. "I hope we'll be able to find em after I pick em up with the loader; they might get buried if the bottom falls out on em"

After spending summers helping my father tear through junk yards I come to know which things to look for when scrapping car bodies.

I could always tell when the gears in his head were turning because he would stop for just a moment and would stare off into space. Then when you least expected it he would shift back to neutral and keep chuggin' away, attentive but always seeming to be in somewhat of a trance.

When lunch time came everyone took time to sit down and reflect on the morning and then make our predictions for the afternoon. For me it was a time to really grasp the complexity of the moment. I would sit there and look at our loaded dump truck and wonder about just how heavy our load of metals was. Sometimes it would come to mind, especially when we were at the mill, that what we are doing is recycling, in a way. But the thought quickly leaves my mind when it's time strap down our load.

"Make sure ya got that ratchet strap hooked on your side!" This I would hear from the opposite side of the dump truck as my father prepared to tighten the straps. Never was I happier to see the dump truck but when it was time to strap down and start our slow ride back to the mill.

This was actually my favorite part of the whole day; riding in the cab of the dump truck gives you a moment of peace to talk without having the constant din of a chop-saw running or the lingering stench of the loader's exhaust.

As we started out of the yard I couldn't help but bring the fact to mind that this was something that most of the people my age would never know about. I would think some kids with their summer jobs and I think about the fact that a kid in New York City would never even probably dream that a kid would have this as a summer job. Not that it's a bad thing or that it's better than others but it's not a job that could be found everywhere either. It just happens to be here.

(untitled)
By Becky C.

For the last few years this place has been a sanctuary, a spot in the universe where everything falls into place, where it's just been me. The circumstances are always changing, but the feeling I get there never does.

The minute I pull into the empty high school parking lot my world rights itself. I sit in my car for a few minutes looking out at the track and the serene early morning emptiness before I head down. When I step onto the slightly springy surface of the track my body wakes up, ready to go. I stretch out on the old chain-link fence, and then I start to run. All thoughts are swept from my mind as I soak in the feeling of my feet hitting the ground and my breath coming out in whooshes. I revel in the solitude, and the only sounds I can hear are the songs coming through my headphones.

I lean into the first curve as it comes up. The curves are the best part. Going around them I feel as though I'm flying. Entering the straight stretch, I stride out, eating up ground as I face toward the newly woken sun. The first few laps that I do I immerse myself in the sensations as I fall into a pace. Hitting the second mile I start facing the issues of the day. Problems never seem too big or so important when I'm moving, and I find solutions with ease. When I start my last lap I've prepared myself and with the last 100 meters coming up I kick up the pace. There's something about sprinting that makes me feel like a cheetah and just about as strong and powerful. I can do anything.

The track in the afternoon is a different beast entirely. Track work-outs with the team are never the joyful occasions my early morning runs are. Then I am catering to someone else's numbers and competing against my fellow athletes. And even though I curse the ground I'm running on I let the movement infuse my body with warmth and happiness.

The company also changes the track, not for better or for worse, just different. Now there's noise where there was quiet and people where there was no one. Mostly I enjoy the people and the friendly competition that comes with it, and even the drama. It helps take my mind off the torture that's awaiting me.

The spring brings track meets where yet more people flood the track and add to the noise. The stress and pressure is palpable. I feel stressed and pressured myself. Then the gun goes off and I'm flying again and it's a combination of my track work-outs and my early morning runs. I run as hard as I can, forcing my legs to stretch farther, my arms to pump faster, and my feet to push off harder. When I reach that last stretch it's only I even though hoards of people are everywhere. I focus only on of the feeling of the track beneath my feet and the rush of air past my ears. That is one of my perfect moments.

But no matter the situation, the time, or the crowd around, I always get the same sense of accomplishment when I leave the track. I feel fulfilled and happy, even after those dreaded track work outs. This place ranges from serene calm to insane pressure, but no matter what I love being there.

Becky C. writes "I wrote about my topic because it is a place where I feel most comfortable and familiar with. My favorite part was 'eating up ground as I face the newly awoken sun.'"

Geography
By Rachel R.

I want to touch everything sharp
And everything soft
I want to feel everything cold
And everything hot

Just to know the difference
Between things
And the chemicals
That make them

To realize that every time
I touch the pavement
I'm connected to everyone else
Who is touching it too

And all the dandelion seeds
That I blow from the stem
Spread all over
To grant more wishes

There is nothing in the world
Like looking at a satellite's image
And realizing that
You're standing under it

Because knowing
Where you're at
And where you are
Are two completely different things

And being alive and living
Are separated by
How much
You appreciate air

Rachel R. has been writing poetry for about two years. Her other interests and hobbies include photography, reading, collecting CDs, and working at From My Shelf Books in Wellsboro, PA. She is currently a junior and plans to attend college in Pennsylvania. She cites some of her main influences as Sarah Kay, Ellen Hopkins, and Taylor Mali. Poems usually start for Rachel while she is journaling. They're about whatever she was thinking a moment before. Geography is really about how everything comes together to form our world and sustain life; and that we should try to thrive and enjoy it.

(untitled)
By Danielle S.

Place, by definition, is a physical environment. To me, a place is anywhere you can go. Depending on the place, you should feel welcomed, loved, and wanted. The more places you go, the more you will learn and see about the world. By learning about the world, you will see that not all places are as welcoming, loving, and friendly as here in The Valley. The Valley consists of Athens, Sayre, and Waverly. It is small, rural, at times boring, but inside of this bantam town we have people that will back you up on your gloomiest of days.

This place has been my home my entire life. Even though there are days where I wish I could move away, to find somewhere more exciting, there is no better place to live than here. I can even see myself raising my own family in this place. It is rural, but you always have the bitty town to go back to. Everyone is connected in some way, you run into an old friend at the local store and can talk for hours catching up.

This devastating flood proves that this Valley can stand together to help make it through. Looking around, you would not recognize the normally cheerful streets. It reminded me of a war zone, with National Guard, and tons of garbage lining the way. Walking down the mud caked sidewalks, smelling the foul air, I see house after house throwing away their soiled memories. If that doesn't make you teary eyed, maybe watching complete strangers help out the victims will. Once you've done all that you can do to help one home, you would move to the next home which looked as if they needed help. With everyone pitching in, the cleanup went much more rapidly.

A place is anywhere you can go, I recommend coming and enjoying the Valley whenever you are around. It is a place where you can feel welcomed and loved. This is an exact definition of what place is to me. I am very fortunate to have grown up and found friends here.

Danielle S. writes "I chose to write about The Valley because it is a humble, warm, inviting place to grow up. You know your neighbors, and you know your neighbor's neighbors. Everyone is connected and it is good to not have unfamiliar faces around. We stand together when things get tough, such as the flood. The sentence 'This devastating flood proves that this Valley can stand together to help make it through' would be my favorite because it speaks the truth about the community I live in. Being small, we can do anything to help each other overcome difficult situations. Seeing that this summer was very touching and heartwarming"

My Place
By Brittani K.

About a half mile from my house is a green bridge. Every evening at sunset I walk to the bridge and sit on a ledge that's connected to the side of the bridge. It's peaceful, quiet, and provides plenty of privacy. I go there to escape from the rest of the world for a little while. I lie on the ledge and listen to the soothing sounds of water falling over rocks while watching the sky change in color.

Sometimes I like to dangle my feet over the edge and wonder if I was to jump if I could land on my feet, even though I know that would be impossible. As I sit on there alone and embrace my surroundings I clear my mind of every irritable thought and just relax. I throw all my worries into the currents and let them simply drift away. Although I know those worries will return shortly after I leave, my mind is clear for the time being. At times I want to throw myself into the current and drift away.

Depending on the day I might stay longer than usual. The warmer the weather, the longer I'll stay. Some days I'll be gone for hours, other days I won't be gone long at all. I like the atmosphere when the sun is setting and the crickets start chirping. These of many things make me not want to ever leave.

As soon as I reach the bridge I turn my phone on silent mode and block out the rest of the world. I don't let anything bother me while I'm there. Not even the biggest concerns I have. I set my mind to think I'm the only person left in the world and ponder deeply on the thought. Sometimes I actually feel as if I am the only one left because it's just so peaceful.

This place is my home away from home. When I feel stressed, overwhelmed, upset, angry, or have no feeling at all I go to the ledge on the bridge. The best part about this place for me is it's mine. No one else knows where I go when I leave. I'm alone and at peace. I'm free to be my real self and I don't have to act in a certain way that I would any other time. The ledge on the green bridge is my sanctuary.

Brittani writes, "I chose to write about the ledge on the green bridge because it was my sanctuary. Some days I would go there to hide, other days just to relax. My favorite part of my work is where I talk about letting all my worries and troubles be washed away."

(untitled)
By Alyssa H.

There was a time when computers could only connect to dial-up. Back then, Mansfield Embroidery was a Pudgie's Pizza, Night and Day was a hardware store, and Wal-Mart had yet to receive its Super title. At that time, I was around five years old, living only a little ways away from the University.

For a while, I thought that every road out of town just led to a dead end after a few miles. I thought the bridge over the Tioga led to the other side of the river and then the road led to a wall. However, while on a trip to Bucktail, at the age of six, I found that this wasn't the case.

As the years passed, I continued to discover just how large the world truly is. I visited other states, Arizona, Florida, New Mexico, with my parents on various family vacations. I saw the ocean, from a bird's eye view, sailing on a cloud of white cotton. I took in the beauty of the countryside in Ireland, the lovely buildings of Wales, visited the majestic and intimidating Edinburgh Castle of Scotland, and compared the hustling bustle of London to a familiar, yet very far away, New York City.

With each trip I took, in both my classes at school and trips with family, the world became larger and larger. There were no dead ends to the world anymore; any dead end in a road could easily be bypassed by another route. However, as the years passed, my home faced changes of its own.

Drilling companies tore up and uprooted trees and grasses, filling the night sky with roaring shades of red. The elementary school caught fire and was rebuilt into a school that will forever be unfamiliar to me. The Farmer and the Dell was shut down and replaced with a Sheetz and a stoplight.

Time has passed and my view of the world, as well as my home, has changed, and yet everything has stayed the same. The world is still the world it was when I was a child and my home, although its features are different, is still my home.

Alyssa H. writes "I once thought my Mansfield was the only place that existed in the world. By writing about my thoughts of the world as a child, I hoped to give readers a look through my eyes. When I wrote 'everything has stayed the same' I'm still that inquisitive girl, just in an older body."

Grandma's Kitchen
By Stephanie P.

A sense of relaxation with an over exceedingly amount of excitement stirs when I smell the delicious aroma of one of my grandmother's homemade pies. The smell is no stranger to me; it is something I have known ever since I can remember. My grandma's kitchen is more than just a place where my belly meets satisfaction, it is a place where jokes are laughed at long and hardily, family is bonded and business is held orderly. The diversity of my grandma's kitchen makes me love being there.

Every morning just as the milker pump shuts off I can almost guarantee that grandma is setting the table for breakfast. She never really is sure of how many people she will be having every morning but she never complains, she improvises. Making new and tasty meals out of the left overs or making extra food for the person that didn't get as much. She never lets anyone leave with an empty stomach. The breakfast she makes is actually no "breakfast" at all; it is more like a dinner. Hearty meals worthy of a farmer's work always completed with a delightful dessert. It is a comforting and nestled feeling I have helping my grandma in the kitchen or just watching her move about gracefully working her magic.

Everyone accumulates in the kitchen after their individualized help on the farm for breakfast. It is a chance for them to warm up, relax, and prepare for their rigorous day of work ahead. It is also a chance for them to share stories of what their day has consisted of or what has been going on with their families. Most everyday someone has a story that makes everyone heave the stress off of their chest and laugh a little. There is barely ever a dull conversation at the table especially at the end of morning chores.

The people who are in grandma's kitchen the most are family. We own a family farm and most of our immediate family lives near grandma's house so it is a good place to reconnect.

Almost all holidays are celebrated with a dinner which includes all of the families. Around Christmas time grandma has all of her grandchildren helping make cookies. I cherish this time to visit and catch up with my cousins. A lot of family memories take place in grandma's kitchen.

A lot of other people besides my family visit my grandmother's kitchen. They are usually there for a variety of reasons, all are very interesting. I love to hear what the people visiting my grandparents have to say. Some are friends of my grandparents looking to catch up and some are business acquaintances ready to pounce on a deal. The range of topics discussed is so interesting to me. I also get a sense of joy to be a sort of host to the people who do not frequently visit my grandmother's kitchen. I love the different personalities that visit and the different agendas of the people who visit my grandma's kitchen.

It feels like everything comes together in my grandmother's kitchen. My worries slip away and my ears open to take in the knowledge that comes from listening to the people who sit around the table. It is where a perfect mix of social skills and technical skills in the kitchen take place. It is an environment that is filled with love and sometimes hatred. Being in my grandma's kitchen keeps me on my toes waiting inquisitively for the next event to occur!

Stephanie P. chose to write about her grandma's kitchen mainly because she loves being there. "It feels like everything comes together in my grandmother's kitchen" is Stephanie's favorite part because everything truly does come together in her grandma's kitchen; it is the heart to the farm and family.

My Place
By Courtney D.

Everyone belongs somewhere. There's always that one place where a person attaches himself. This place could be on a stage with costumes and lights dancing across their eyes. It could be nurturing abused children in a hospital or navigating a plane through wispy clouds. It could be defending someone in a courtroom or creating a masterpiece carving.

These are places where people just know that they are meant to be. But for me, it's different. I don't think my heart is tied to just a single place. My heart belongs in a hundred different places. Where I belong, my senses are the most intense and on edge, where everything seems louder, more vivid, and just feels different. These senses reveal the places that I truly belong.

My place is in music. I can hear notes singing their harmonies as my fingers dance on black and white keys. A part of me belongs in a place of melodies and lyrics. But my heart is a broken puzzle and music is only a single piece.

The volleyball court is not usually a place I associate with belonging, but I can literally feel the competition, physical strain, and edge all pulsing in my veins and I know that it too fits somewhere in my puzzled heart.

Nature is something I thrive on. I can sit in a field for hours and do nothing but look at the sky. Looking isn't even the right word. I'm feeling it. I'm feeling starlight cross my irises and I'm breathing in wind that has passed nations not known to me. Grass and mountains and snow and oceans. My senses wrap around such things, and these images breathe inside a jagged jigsaw piece.

Writing might take several puzzle pieces in itself. Writing doesn't belong to me. I belong to writing. I fell in love with words and stories before I could even make sense of their meanings. Poetry and lyrics jump from my fingers. Ideas flutter like moth wings in charcoal letters and I can feel my place in such a lined canvas. Scratches of a pen, crumpled up paper, and black ink spilling across in words. My senses sew more pieces together.

Faith is the bordering pieces to my puzzle, the part that holds the rest together. My place lies within my beliefs. Music -my worship. The court -my battle. Nature -the Creation. Writing -my journey. Over the years my heart fell for serving and all my goals began to change.

A sense of place isn't a single spot on the map or a solitary idea. Such a place is a hundred unique pieces sewn together to display the whole picture. These senses of belonging piece themselves together to depict a place of the future.

My senses can depict a future, a future where my place lies in Africa. Music of handcarved instruments. A battle of disease and heartache. An endless beauty of creation. A place where I can write about my fears and grasp fingertips of hurting people.

This is my sense of what place really means. Every single thing in a person's life pulls you to a place where everything you love and belong to can be sent into motion. A place where you can simply breathe and blink and live and know that this is where you really belong.

A Sense of Place
By Anthony R.

You sit alone

In the room

Two groups sit in front of you

One group is the popular kids

With nice clothes and fancy cars

The other is the normal kids

With average clothes and grades not up to par

You must choose one, and the other will disappear

You sit and wait, with a sense of fear

Your friends in both groups wait and cheer

What will you choose?

What is your sense of place?

Anthony R. is 18 years old and a student at Mansfield Jr. Sr. High School. Anthony writes "This poem is a personal story about how I feel everyday about the two groups of friends I have in my school. My favorite part is the ending because it leaves the reader thinking who will he choose in end."

(untitled)
By Rachel J.

It was the same dull routine every day that was killing the man. He would wake up, go to work, and return to his apartment late at night to get some sleep before repeating the process. The endless cycle robbed him of his energy and seemingly of his personality as well, but life, even as it stays the same, is constantly changing. There are always new opportunities and choices. Everyone has a chance for change, even someone such as the man on his dismal trek. All it takes is a small detail that can lead to a realization of the situation, which, in turn, could make the victim conscious of a choice.

The man was walking through the crowded sidewalks on his way to work as usual when he stopped. It was amazing that no one bumped into him when he suddenly came to a standstill, but the river of people just walked around him and carried on. He had seen a flash of red out of the corner of his eye. It was a small explosion of color in the grey-black world he lived. It made him stop and look. It was a little red leaf scampering along in the wind on the sidewalk across the street.

It was autumn. He realized this with a jolt. He barely noticed the seasons anymore, they all blurred together with the endless days of working. He realized that he couldn't remember any specific event in the cycle of days, or even differentiate one day from another. He found that he had been too busy to live. He felt the despair of a wasted life as the realizations washed over him one after another. He discovered that he did not like the direction his life was going and wanted to change it immediately. Then he saw all the people around him, all going to dull jobs of their own and made a decision.

The man pulled himself together and told himself that he was being absurd. He shrugged off the last wandering thoughts in his mind and resumed walking to work as usual. This was life.

Everyone had dull patches here and there. He would simply carry on like everyone else as just another drop in the river. The man reasoned with himself in this manner all the way to his desk in his office where he set himself down ready to start the work that would take him to his grave.

The cycle would continue uninterrupted as the man filled a place not meant for him. He would just continue, numb to the world, and live an unfulfilled life. He stared at the piles of chores and responsibilities stacked in neat piles on his desk and sighed. He stood up and walked down the hall to his boss's office about to call a sick day and give himself a break, but when he opened his mouth he found himself announcing that he did not want to occupy a place that was not his. As he continued, he realized that his words were true and that he would find the place meant for him in the vast world. With those thoughts, Felix Gray declared his resignation.

Rachel J. writes "I'm just like any other kid in high school; I think I'm different from everyone else, but we all know that I'm the same as every other teenager on the planet. I'm way too busy doing everything and nothing at the same time while contemplating my place in the universe and distracting myself with electronic devices. I could mention that I'm in an excessive amount of extracurricular activities, a big fan of all books in general, and a complete know-it-all, but no one wants to hear about all that nonsense. I am quite similar to the main character in my essay and must constantly remind myself to live my life, as everyone should." Rachel says she chose her topic "because I wanted something reasonably different from the stereotypical takes on the suggested theme and I wanted to make a point that many people could identify with."

The Rape of Marcellus
By Alyson Leach

Teasingly the affair blooms
Money is exchanged from hand to hand
Titillation soon follows
The relationship begins to pulse and throb
Wallet and heart pound like a drum
Drilling commences.
Thrusting inward with fluids
That stimulate
The moment of ecstasy is fleeting
The momentary giddiness of it all
Then
Violating, infringing, assaulting.
Scars, physical and internal remain
The treasure explored, captured and conquered
The victor vanquishes,
Leaving
The victim a
Pitted vacant shell.

Keep on Truckin'
By Jane Spohn

"Want to come on tomorrow's run, Kid?"

Those words were music to my ears. There was no better place in the world than next to my dad in his Mack cabover, hauling something to somewhere, that bull dog hood ornament leading the way. Mom would help me pack a bag. A book, a notebook and pencil. .. unnecessary things when I got to sit up high in an air ride seat next to my dad. Secretly I hoped my sister wouldn't want to come along. Three is a crowd. Yes, taking turns lying in the bunk on your belly peeking out the windshield over the huge dash full of knobs and buttons was fun too, but nothing was better than being the copilot.

Climbing into the truck was part of the enjoyment. I felt like a mountain climber as I pulled myself up the steep steps with the help of the chrome grab handles. Once at my perch, the world looked different. I could see everything. I knew we were big, maybe the biggest thing on the road that day. Power surged through my body as the truck lurched out of the yard and onto the highway. My senses were heightened and on overload. Explaining the view from a cabover is hard to do. The road rolls right out in front of your eyes, as there is no hood and engine to get in your way. It is really you and the road as we hammered down the highway. As a child it was even more amazing than when I saw Niagara Falls for the first time, and my next ride would again be just as amazing.

The radio provided music for our journey, but the mysterious voices on the CB were even more melodious. CB jargon takes some time to learn, but after asking Dad several questions I'd just sit back and listen and get the gist of conversations. When asking about road and weather conditions, little phrases were added to the beginning and endings of questions or replies like "come back" or "copy". The language was musical and lively. So many different voices filled the airway with so many things to say. It never once crossed my mind that being an over the road driver must be lonely. That CB was the only thing they had until the next truckstop. To me it was the best toy ever and I waited patiently until Dad would let me push in the button and reply to someone on the other end. A little girl riding with her daddy draws some attention. Drivers would wave and smile and say a little hello when we passed other trucks on the highway. I quickly was dubbed "Slick Chick" as my CB handle and used it a bit shyly at first, gaining confidence with each verbal transaction. You could catch me asking, "This is Slick Chick, what's your 10-20?"

Of course nothing can be perfect, and I would find that out each trip when we pulled into our destination. Most places had rules and regulations that made passengers stay in the truck at the loading dock. Dad would back in, set the air brakes with a huge whoosh of air, and tell me he'd be back in a few minutes as he grabbed the paperwork and climbed down his side of the rig. It felt like hours as I waited, wanting to watch the forklift unload the pallets off the truck and to see what other trucks were delivering. Loading docks were teeming with excitement and I missed every bit of it sitting in what used to be the greatest seat in the world.

Finally, along came Dad, whistling a tune as he climbed much more gracefully than me up into the cab. Seeing him next to me again washed away all of the disappointment of being left alone. Sometimes he even had candy from a vending machine to share with me. What disappointment? All was well in that Mack truck! The road seemed shorter on the ride back home. My time with Dad was counting down and the one-of-a-kind feeling of being in that truck would soon be over. We sang along to Alabama on the radio, talked with truckers from across the USA, and wound our way back over and through the mountains, just him and me.

Mom would be waiting with dinner on the table. My sister would ask questions about where we had been. I would tell my friends in school about the trip. But no words could ever capture the magic of the ride, the road rolling out before me, the music of the mysterious CB voices, and the honor of sitting next to the greatest guy in the universe.

Jane Spohn is a 7th grade reading, math, and science teacher at Williamson Middle School. Married to a truck driver and mechanic, she hopes her four children have fond memories of growing up around trucks. She remembers that her dad spent most of his time away from home working, so those times she got to be with him, especially alone with him, were cherished. There is truly no better feeling in the world than spending time with the greatest guy in the universe, especially as the king and princess of the open road.

Covered Bridge
By RG Wilcox

He gathered me with work-gloved hands and carried me in his flannel-clad arms. I was a barn, collapsed and long forgotten. I was taken just over a mile away. He stacked my parts in organized piles on the soft, green grass beside a creek that barely trickled.

To the east lay a small pasture, which would become a lawn. A grove of hickory and sycamore trees stood across the creek to the west. He used rocks from the creek bed to form the headwalls along the banks where I would be anchored. The rough-hewn timbers spanned the width. Silo staves became the decking. The weathered boards were measured and sawn to create board-and-batten siding. Two windows looked out on the sides, north and south. A short approach on each end with handrails served as the final tethers to solid ground. Tin roofing with sunset-colored streaks along the ribs provided my crowning glory.

His wife brought sandwiches and together they admired his progress. Their two children, a boy and a girl, ran in the lawn and splashed in the creek in their little black rubber boots. They scrambled over every inch of me as I arose. When I was completed, they ran to the woodlot and back, gathering leaves, sticks, and flowers. They'd drop them from the upstream window, race to the other side, and watch as their treasures emerged from my shadow and floated off. I was the first structure he built on the land they called their own.

Hickory Grove, as the woodlot became known, was furnished with a picnic table and a stone fire ring. The grandparents came, and the son wrote a speech to commemorate the first picnic and campfire there. Many more gatherings followed. Family, friends, and wildlife all trotted across my floor.

In summer, the buttercups and multi-flora roses blossomed along the creek. I watched with pride as a house, garage, and gazebo were built on the rise to the east. In autumn, I delighted as squirrels and chipmunks dined while perched on my window sills. I safeguarded a screech owl that roosted in my rafters. I blushed and beamed as the daughter had her pictures taken with me. In winter, I stood stalwart as snow was measured by the blanket on my roof and the drifts in my entrance. In spring, I anticipated the arrival of violets in purple and white that colored the woodlot floor. I gave audience to peepers, songbirds and crickets as they sang harmoniously, with the rumble of [dump] trucks on the dirt road beyond providing bass. I was the symbol of this utopia.

One September, the rains came in torrents. They carved out hillsides and washed out roads. Then they came for me. The angry mobs of water amassed upstream, uprooting trees and disinterring boulders. They clawed out the rocks from my headwalls then pummeled me with debris. I was strong, but they were many and stronger. My roof was tossed to rest near the top of the bank. Chunks of my sides and flooring were hauled downstream for gruesome souvenirs. Errant pieces were discarded as if playthings, no longer amusing. In the gray dawn, my approaches on both sides lay pointing in the direction I had gone.

The modest streambed lay ripped into a chasm. The banks were scoured and raw. The woodlot, now inaccessible, felt like a forbidden land. The rotting picnic table tilted against the trunk of a tree. The fire pit lay buried beneath layers of silt and leaf litter.

There was shock, tears, and finally sad acceptance. The one who made me donned his work gloves and gathered what parts of me could be found.

A larger fire ring made of steel now lies in the lawn closer to the house. The children have grown and gone off to college. My future is uncertain. For now, my crowning glory remains intact; resting beside stacked and organized piles, on the soft, green grass, by a creek that once again barely trickles.

R. G. Wilcox writes and resides in Canton, Pennsylvania. "Covered Bridge" was written to illustrate how a sense of place can evoke deep emotion. The author likes the sentence: "The angry mobs of water amassed upstream, uprooting trees and disinterring boulders."

Attic Heir-looms
By Jessica Spencer

"A place for everything, everything in its place."
Benjamin Franklin

My Grandmother weaved rag rugs. Her attic was full of peoples' hand-me downs that were too tight, stained, or outdated to appear in public anymore. Boxes bulged with layers and layers of different fabric blends. When you entered the small quaint space of her attic, tucked off of the middle bedroom, generations of styles could be dated by peeling back the stacks of clothes that gathered in the saturated cardboard. As grandchildren, we used these clothes to play dress up. We didn't mind that they smelled musty and were topped with dust.

When it was just my Grandmother and I, I loved to help her cut the clothes into long two-inch wide strips. I sat on her living room floor for hours and ripped apart pairs of blue jeans, old slacks, and shirts. When I accumulated a massive pile, I brought the heap over to the sewing room and watched my Grandmother vigorously sew the strips into long strands. Zzzzzt, rest, zzzzzt, rest, zzzzzt, rest. Until all of these strips strung together and coiled like a snake at the bottom of her chair. Finally, I wound these long lines of colors and patterns into balls full of possibilities.

They say another person's rags are another person's riches. My Grandmother would take these balls of cloth and begin to weave them back and forth until a rug appeared on her loom. The loom sat on her sun porch nuzzled in the corner opposite of the entry door. There were a few things we knew not to touch in her house; the Avon collection from years of selling make-up and perfume, the organ, and the loom. I never remember any of us grandchildren having too much of a problem with these rules. It was a given.

When she began to weave, the loom had a beat and rhythm as she slid the cloth wand back and forth and banged the long strips of cloth into place. Long, wooden pedals at her feet alternated the direction of the weave. Swish, swish, bang, bang. Swish, swish, bang, bang. Swish, swish, bang, bang. On and on the sound echoed off the small windowed walls while I sat and watched trying to comprehend the sequence of events.

All of my families' homes were filled with these rugs and some were the direct result of the clothing that we dropped off. My Grandmother filled many orders for local friends and families. She also sold them at the local craft fairs. I followed along sometimes and noticed people pick her out amongst the other vendors to peruse her rugs that were displayed on drying racks or rolled up and sorted by color on a nearby table. I listened to them pay her compliments, and gladly hand over their money for her work. These rugs covered hardwood floors, tile, and laminate. They helped to cushion feet and protect against a cold stinging floor. They decorated rooms with a myriad of blues from denim or a multi-colored splash to fit anywhere our hearts desired.

I have a few rag rugs remaining of my Grandmother's that she kept in her home. When she passed away I knew that this was one keepsake that I wished to treasure and save. They are in use as she would want them to be. My favorite is a solid red runner with white trim that greets us in the entryway of the morning room. I cringe when I see a tatter or stain develop, knowing that this rug is a piece that keeps me woven to my place with my Grandmother.

Jessica Spencer writes "My family and I spent a lot of time growing up at my Grandma's house between the holidays and just hanging out. She was the epitome of what a Grandma should be. I think about her often and the time I spent in her quaint place in Arnot, Pennsylvania."

Memories
By Nina Wells

Memories are like waves in the ocean, always moving, ebbing, and flowing. As I have gotten older I seem to notice this phenomenon much more. I remember a memory from my childhood quite differently than my sister. I clearly remember it was her fault that the back door window shattered into a thousand pieces as she threw it closed to keep me out. My sister remembers this event as my fault; the window in the door broke because I put my foot in the way of her closing the door. Sometimes it isn't the perspective on the memory, but the importance of a memory. We have all heard someone tell an inspiring story of how one small exchange between two people changed their lives for the better, like "you can be anything you want to be" ,and the person decides right then and there that this is absolutely true and decides they will be the first astronaut to land on the moon. The funny thing is the person who made the statement doesn't even remember saying this to the other person. I have a memory that I feel encompasses all these qualities into one and has changed meaning for me as I have gotten older.

Years ago when I was the around the age of twelve my family and I lived on a small farm. There were eight of us kids and as most of you know farming is not the most lucrative career choice out there. My mother and father were always looking for ways to make ends meet and feed the hordes of starving children. Down the road from our house about a mile, setting back from the road was an old abandon farmhouse that had an apple orchard. Every fall the whole family would head down to the orchard to pick apples to make applesauce and every spring the yard area would be completely covered with daffodils. As soon as they were blooming, I was heading down the road to pick as many as I could possibly carry to brighten up the house. All of the children were told never to enter the house. "One wrong move and the whole house could come down around your ears," my father would say. I don't know how the rest of my siblings felt, but I know that statement alone made me want to run right up the rickety front porch steps and run in and explore every single nook and cranny in that old house up stairs and down! I can say with all honesty though I never did go inside that house.

Although I didn't go in the house, nothing could stop me from spending hours just daydreaming about who used to live in that grand old house. The house was quite large and all the paint was wore off but, you could tell at one time the house was white. I always imagine that the house must have glowed at night with the white paint shining out into the night. I would dream of how the owners must have been rich to be able to build such a beautiful house. I just always knew that there must have been beautiful furniture with everything polished to perfection. That house must have had everything we didn't have and much more.

As I have gotten older and I would hope to say wiser, my perspective on this memory has changed. The old farm house with the apple orchard and daffodils that would splash their brilliant yellow color through the shadows of the gloomiest day are long gone. I still think about this memory, but now with more of a tinge of sadness mixed with the goodness. I miss the time spent as a family gathering the apples and the smile my mother would give me as I came in the door with my arms loaded with daffodils. I don't think so much of what the old house must have looked like in its glory days. I think about how hard it must have been for the owners of that house to make it and what tragic thing must have happened to make them leave such a beautiful place.

I am always amazed at how the thoughts of a child and that of an adult can be so different. How amazed I am that one memory can change as your life experiences change you. I guess when you think about our memories and ourselves we are ever changing like the waves in the ocean.

Nina Wells writes "I would like to think the reason my memory has changed throughout the years is because I have grown as person." Nina's favorite line is "I always imagine that the house must have glowed at night with the white paint shining out into the night."

(untitled)
By Tom Wells

Twenty one years seems like eternity when you are a teenager. As you advance in life and reflect back it seems to have flown by quickly. Twenty one years ago I looked forward to spending all of my time on the mountain. My dad and I would fish, hunt, take long walks, and enjoy rides on the back roads. He would tell me stories of when he was at an earlier age. At times these stories were very boring for a thirteen year old like me.

My mountain time was every weekend that we were able to get up the no winter maintenance road to the cabin. We often arrived late Friday night and left Sunday afternoon. The cabin had no running water just a spring to get water from and an outdoor privy. We heated with a woodstove to which I perfected building fires in. There was electricity with an old radio that was on during most of our stay.

Cold weather was an excellent time to sit and read while listening to the radio. Every season marked a change in activities. We always started trout season on opening day in April. Dad and I would fish all spring and summer whenever we could find time. During other times we enjoyed target practice with various guns. My dad always had advice on everything and he was very strict on gun safety. During the summer we used to cut and split wood at different spots that loggers had harvested.

October would arrive and the leaves would change and small game season opened. We spent a lot of time in the woods and dad inspected my every move. November meant Thanksgiving and the Monday after marked the first day of antlered season in 1990. Dad showed me the tricks of deer hunting and we saw quite a few doe, but no buck in those first two weeks. The antlerless season opened for 3 days and we hunted the first two with no luck.

The New Year came and the mountain was in a different season again. We started fishing in April and continued on through when I had time around my busy schedule. We spent the Independence Day weekend on the creek fishing. We really enjoyed that weekend and made plans to go out the following weekend. That weekend never came for Dad. He died of a massive heart attack that week. I did not fish again that year.

That fall I was at the cabin one frosty morning and that was when I realized all of the beauty of nature that Dad had been telling me about. That morning the fog was dense near the ground with the sun shining bright above. The leaves were in full color and I stood there and enjoyed the tranquility with my Dad. I was fourteen that morning and vowed to enjoy the nature on the mountain as much as possible.

My mountain has been a special place for me through the years. I hunted, hiked, and visited whenever I could and Dad was there every step of the way. I gave up fishing all together and put those days with the memories of Dad. The years have gone by quickly and I am now married with two children. My daughter is 14 and my son is 10. My daughter does not enjoy the outdoors as much as my son and I find myself telling him the stories that Dad told me.

Hunting season of 2010 my son Dylan hunted with me and my older brother, Mike and I both harvested our first buck ever. I have a picture of Dylan and me on that special day and it hangs on our living room wall. Dad was not in that picture, but he was with all of us on the mountain that day.

I look back through the last 20 years, and think of how the mountain has changed. Telephone lines were ran to the cabins in the mid 90's and cell phones with texting are everywhere today. There have been several storms and trees that Dad and I hunted by are gone today. The new gas boom in the Marcellus shale has had the largest impact on my mountain. Hills have been leveled and trees removed for pipelines and gas well pads.

I wonder where we will be in twenty more years and if it was worth the money to destroy my mountain and my memories. No one else will enjoy the beauty that Dad and I have enjoyed.

Tom Wells writes "I grew up in rural Pennsylvania and this story was based on true events of my life. I have enjoyed every step of the way and it has gone by so quickly. The one sentence that means the most to me in the story is when I 'enjoyed the tranquility with my Dad'"